BETWEEN THE ROWS

BETWEEN THE ROWS

NANCY K. JENTSCH

poems

SHANTI ARTS PUBLISHING

BRUNSWICK, MAINE

Between the Rows

Published by Shanti Arts Publishing
Designed by Shanti Arts Designs

Cover image by Pixabay on pexels.com (CC0 1.0)
Universal (CC0 1.0) Public Domain Dedication

Shanti Arts LLC
193 Hillside Road
Brunswick, Maine 04011
shantiarts.com

Printed in the United States of America

ISBN: 978-1-956056-54-9 (softcover)

Library of Congress Control Number: 2022947317

*To my husband, Philip Enzweiler,
whose ever-patient love
has made it possible to live
between the rows.*

Contents

OVERNIGHT

EVERY DAY HAS SOMETHING IN IT

Acknowledgements

I gratefully acknowledge the following publications in which a version of these poems originally appeared, some with different titles.

Amethyst Review: "Evening Mantra"

Black Moon Magazine: "Beethoven and Spellbound Deer"; "Into Uncertainty"; "Redbuds, April 2020"; and "Slide Rule Diptych"

Blinders: "In Gaza" (as "One Concert Grand in Gaza")

Bonfire(s): "Left Behind"

Eclectica: "Madonna Mends Her Own Heart"; "Night's Crown, 2020" (as "Winter's Ills"); *"Sammeltassen"*; and "Survivors"

For a Better World: Poems and Drawings on Peace and Justice: "Managua por la mañana"

Gyroscope Review: "Bucket List" and "Overnight"

Kentucky Philological Review: "Weightless Wish" and "Which Call, Which Kiss"

Lexington Poetry Month Blog: "Between the Rows, 2020" (as "Between the Rows"); "My Son Moves Out"; and "Worries' Beads"

Out of Anonymity: "The Sorcery of Sapphire Skies"

Panoply: "Dawnlessness" and "A Kind of Nothing Is Prominently There Instead"

Soul-Lit: "Nana's Mirror"

Star 82 Review: "All Brains and Thumbs"

Thimble Literary Magazine: "Puppy Meets Pieter Bruegel (1525–1569)"

Zingara Poetry Review: "Every Day Has Something in It"

"On an analog walk" (as "Analog Walk") was published in *A Walk with Nature: Poetic Encounters that Nourish the Soul*, ed. Michael Moats, et al. (University Professors Press, 2019).

"Butterfly ballads" was published in *Trees in a Garden of Ashes: Poetry of Resilience*, ed. James P. Wagner (Local Gems Press, 2020).

"Ohio River Field Station" was published in *Riparian: Poetry, Short Prose, and Photographs Inspired by the Ohio River*, ed. Sherry Cook Stanforth (Dos Madres Press, 2019).

"All Brains and Thumbs" and "*Managua por la mañana*" appeared in the chapbook *Authorized Visitors* (Cherry Grove Collections, 2017).

"Pop-pop" received Honorable Mention in the Ohio Poetry Day Contest, 2015.

Several poems in this collection were inspired by the work of artist Bianca Artopé. Her work may be seen at www.artope.com or by scanning the QR code on the left.

I am grateful to the Kentucky Foundation for Women for support in preparing this collection through an Arts Enrichment Grant (2020) and two Hopscotch House Retreats (2019 and 2020).

A special thanks is due to Pauletta Hansel for mentoring me throughout the manuscript process and giving me wings. I would also like to acknowledge my poetry mates Donelle Dreese, Karen George, and Taunja Thomson, who workshopped first drafts of most of these poems with me; and my sister, Lynda, who lovingly reads my poems, encourages me, and answers my many questions.

UNEXPECTED

Bucket List

Spend time in a barn
where hay is stacked

for a whiff of last spring's blooms
and next week's milk

Walk outside in the rain
long enough for hope to wash you

in water charged by lightning
and drawn to its ground

Take a lap around the park
at half your normal speed

See a burl you've passed before
imagine the kaleidoscope within

Consider the perfect sphere
of a Michigan blueberry

before it caresses tongue and palette
sweet with a late summer finish

Sit by the four o'clocks
to watch them unfurl

when they join night's first sighs
exhaling hue and scent

Puppy Meets Pieter Bruegel (1525–1569)

What scents linger
by the creek
where you stop and sniff
cataloging
skunks, toads, voles
whose ways crossed here
when darkness last crowded
this narrow valley?
Their traces make
your wet, jet-black nose
quiver even now.

Bruegel could capture
it all on one canvas
reducing night's saga
to a synchronous collage
dark's secrets forced
into two dimensions.

But your pleasure
blooms unbarred
the moonlit moments
mapped
by their bouquet.

Landlocked Luck

When starlings cartwheel
and thunder, I think of beaches
and blue-green waves, tugged too
like puppets on see-through strings
performing show and encore
show and encore.
And I wonder if those whose feet
tickle sand think of starling
swarms when their waves crest and crash
crest and crash?
Or am I lucky living landlocked
by bluegrass and limestone
pinning a second stanza,
blue-green, to the poem the starlings
paint above our hills?

Purple Tights

A sale bin bubbles with tights
I plunge for impractical purple
but surface with basic gray

though the adventure of purple
would have had the same price
the same leg-hugging warmth

but been seasoned with a pinch
of spring's lavender promise—
an unconsidered ROI

Chi

Try this right now.
Put your palms parallel
but not quite touching.
Feel space and energy
amaze you with their pulse.

No need to trek deserts
traverse icecaps
when what you seek
nestles between your fingers
springs from the balls of your feet.

Day's Deceit

Sun's mirage of warmth pools
our valley this March midday.
Pink-cheeked promise gusts
from river bottoms, goads
old brush into retreat.
When dusk runs late
peepers tsk a know-it-all taunt.
In evening's chill we heat
and spice cider, pop corn,
then sneak through moonbeams—
deceived by day's sleight of hand—
fetch peat pots from shed,
sow seeds of belief
in summer's salsa.

Fear's Fever

Does fear circle us—
a fever of stingrays
dervishes roiling the water
swirling round inferno's core
tails barbed for battle?

If we would only
lower our fists
unfold our fingers
dip them into the fray
we might happen upon
the silky otherworldliness
of a stingray's back
seeking strokes
despite our alien nature.

Slide Rule Diptych

I

The slide rule quivered from Pop-Pop's hands
its hairline calculations began to stumble.
He stared, wordless and stubble-cheeked,
backed for years by his Windsor chair.

We groped in his twilight's tar for a key
to wind his neurons till they ticked again,
our only clues the blurred glass negative
of a tall man proudly dwarfed by garden's corn,
the dusty violins he bought and sought
to copy for the love of their song.

II

My age-spotted hands now glide the bar
behind the slide rule's cracked window
reach beyond the faded hairline
winding time back to our first meeting.

At this same desk but in a room where walls
painted orange swaddled an aura of love-worn
stuffed animals, matches and sealing wax
that only the budding verses of teenage song could unlock,
my hands had touched the complexity
of this keen mind Parkinson's had pocketed.

intrusion I

artwork by Bianca Artopé, 2017

flow of thin tin roofs
crests below
    din of hotels
    casinos
    amusements
could one day
    paralyze traffic
    overturn the sprawling
    bed of privilege
    and its gentrified spreadsheet

watch while
you still can see
purple dissolve to pink
as sunset paints
her blue-gray voile

Unexpected

Parkinson's robbed me of Pop-pop
when I was ten
a girl in frills and anklets
smile barely smudged
by death's theft
Behind the funeral home
we cousins played
not learning till later
the doleful dance steps
of mourning

Even now
when shock
upends
I crouch
in business casual
as if behind
the playground slide
eyes closed
counting
to one hundred

Survivors

Last fall
I weeded and mulched
the garden's back corner
Thought I'd saved
myself an April task

But spring struck
armed with wet vengeance
and the first dry day
sees violets, vetch
Virginia creeper
all latched lush
to the mulched patch
Crabgrass chases
the yarrow
from its treasured
center, lost but for
a few ferny
fronds surviving
at the edges

fragile as the frayed
threads that slipped limp
through my fingers
when the baby was lost
the sky shattered

Madonna Mends Her Own Heart

Colors jump from their wheel
brush her blue, yellow, red

She holds her torn heart
stitches wounds punched

by nails and sword
right cross left cross right

If hung, gilt-framed
on nursery walls

she would radiate agency
a message sweeter

than any honey-clad tale
that walks the Hundred Acre Wood

Cup's Crack

I don't want to wrestle figures
to reckon the number of days
I have ambled motherless

how much warmth her needles
never knitted, how many crusts
she neither rolled nor fluted.

No ruler need size
the crack in my cup
where sips of hours' nectar

grieve in silent seeping.
Neither years nor reason
have mended the cleft

where mourning's dew
tends to beget angry tumors
that grow—random, grotesque.

Though lifeblood leaked
can petal instead
into rosebud's ephemeral

perfection.

hanging hopes from chandeliers II

artwork by Bianca Artopé, 2016

carefully draped
curtains
frame hallway
leading
to arranged flowers—
finish-line prize

untouched chairs
in foreground
ignore
three boys sleeping
huddled barefoot
pulses hopeful
smudging
villa's polished opulence
despite matching
its striped décor
with musty shirts

Sammeltassen

When I rinse her *Sammeltassen*,
fluted floral cups gentle in my hand,
Mimmie comes to mind,
a girl too tattered to have gathered
such fine prizes for a dowry.

She wed her new-world love
empty-handed but happy as ever a bride
who straddled a threshold
with a hopeful load of *Sammeltassen*.

Only after her children grew
peace rooted in her mother's homeland
could the *Queen Elizabeth* sail her east
to acquire the cups plates saucers—*Sammeltassen*
her past had ransomed and my hands attend.

Without Delay

If we had waited any longer
the now of our moment
would have already rustled
past, gowned in mourning
no longer able to lean
our weariness on tree trunks
stitch our torn seams
with cloud-spun thread
stroke our bruises with breeze's
balm. And see—even though
we didn't delay, this moment
already cloaks for its journey

though not before the day's bellflower
opens another five-pointed bloom

Rose-gold keepsake

rings my finger. Its prongs
swaddle a chipped ruby that sparkles
with questions of whether Nana
treasured the ring, how it came to be mine
in its timeworn velvet case,
why I wear it without fail.
Its loyal circle binds
me to her ringless hands, knotted
with arthritis, lavished with Bengay.
Hands that had stitched X after X
on a vast tablecloth, set on conquering
the threat of stiffened impotence.
Now I walk while joints moan,
twirl the ring, head around the bend.

On an analog walk

no thumbs drum
no earbuds pulse
no Fitbits tick

but champagne breeze prickles skin
birdsong bounces between wires
the bend ahead promises Oz
musky smells and sapsucker's tapping
braid with the shade of a stand of trees

Deer's stare
salamander's surprise
freeze time
so that
now
gains depth and breath
to sustain beyond
drumming pulsing ticking
at walk's end

INTO UNCERTAINTY

Virtual Sleep

Grounded at the bus stop
earplugged into virtuality
she's oblivious to raucous
calls of geese
angled to scissor sky—
masked ambassadors sing
of new season
glide wise
keen on winging home.

Will she and her pals ever hear
the honking that heralds flying Vs
care that selfless leaders know
to peel back to the ranks
feel the pulse
      of spring and fall
      north and south?

It is virtual sleep
to sense solely what spins
within your skin
synapses silenced
eyes and ears turned inward.

And then the briars grow
seal the body's fortress
till nothing startles, wakes
not a kiss or even the geese
still plotting their course
          spring and fall
            north and south.

Into Uncertainty

"...*what matters is whether we have the courage*
to venture forth despite the uncertainty of acclaim."
—from *A Gentleman in Moscow* by Amor Towles

At the moment the concerto begins
we don't know how stirring it will be.
Nor on seeing the first snowflake

how thick a coat of snow will fall
A flap of wings can't assure us
that the fledgling will succeed

and not drop to the patient cat.
But without a first snowflake,
an initial flight, an opening chord

inertia wins and tomorrow surrenders,
becomes like the moment a candle's wick
comes to grief. What could have been bright

bleeds to ash.

Dawnlessness

I was born into a room
where the window
leans east
Sun drenches dreams
in summer-squash yellow
dispels whatever darkness
had draped with its chill
On an easel lit with honeysuckle
dawn quilts a counterpane of dew
sings with rooster's gusto

This year I've been moved to a room
where the window
tends west
sunsets beckon with mottled rose quartz
suddenly infused with neon
in a sky that glows turquoise
before darkening
behind stars that pin me
to this chill
of dawnless days

Night's Crown, 2020

Twilight's first snowflake falls
fate-laden yet light
      as a virus.
Its crystals stitch
jigsaw patterns
      sing unknown strains.
Flurries build
from cloud to ground
      as if exhaled unmasked.
Flakes dust obsidian sky
like diamonds
      studding night's crown.
Will spring's sunrise mutter
hungry to cure
      winter's ills?

Between the Rows, 2020

Stains wash out easily
29 years after these
infant sweaters saw use.

Wool dries while Covid's fog
thickens, and my thoughts fly,
land in London, June 1940.

There bombers would soon
sully the sky, hammer
panic onto death and grief

while young women, aglow
behind blackout curtains,
stripped stains from tiny clothes.

Under masks, we too fold hope—
my daughter-in-law and I—
between the knitted rows.

hanging hopes from chandeliers I

artwork by Bianca Artopé, 2016

I

like prisms
hang lives
clever thoughts
pulsing blood
potential
to love

II

like prisms
hang lives
quivering limbs
smelly wounds
unattained
desires

III

polished opulence
sneers, veiled stairways
deceive, lamps
hoard light

IV

lives that dangle
like prisms
from ship
will
tip
it

V

but the villa
is vacant
no one
but the hopeful
will notice

Myrica Pensylvanica

A pair of bayberry candles
flanks the strictly striped
sofa of an orderly childhood
But nothing from years
of pristine packed lunches
and weekly cleaning lists
survives to neatly comb and braid
maturity's matted strands

Even recalling scoops
of hand-cranked ice cream
licked and laughed over
rides on salted Florida waves
bayberry-scented evenings

can't ungnarl my days'
knotted paths
dotted with bayberry shrubs
grown green
watered by weeping

Fall from Grace

This day slipped from my week's needle
like a perfect purl. Dawn's goldfinches

besieged the feeder, pairs of downy
and red-bellied woodpeckers feasted

on suet sequined with seeds and nuts.
In thirty-two rows not one stitch

was dropped. A pair of pots steeped
spiced tea and pillowed dreams. Snow's

hush stoked the stove's whispering flames.
A midday crowd of cranes cried

on their southbound flight. Now doves
flutter like falling leaves, coo dusk's refrain.

What will become of us
when all the birds are gone,

when earth's days tangle and riot, dreams
pale and dusk bestows mere darkness?

intrusion III

artwork by Bianca Artopé, 2017

I

City lights
intrude on night sky
lake sashays
to beat
of order
money
might

II

Straight lines
angled symmetry
could lull to sleep
except that

III

dabs of lives
from slighted suburbs
hang on railings
pose
like paint on palettes
waiting

IV

to lead
the dance

Beethoven and Spellbound Deer

Aware their fate awaits, necks twist
whole-note eyes tacked to source
of scent or sound. Rumens pause
their cud-making task. Hooves soak
in dew from fog that hushes
the waking hillside. Doe's bones
hold breeze at bay. Young buck
pins risk of courage to chest.
This is Beethoven's kind of drama
when senses and muscles bond
in breath-held silence.
It could break in an escape
of thundering haste or as a head
bound for grass and taste of acorn.

Pop-pop

Standing tall beside
cornstalks that dwarf you
fixed on a glass negative
delivered from the barn's musty darkroom
I glimpse the man
they told me you were
(because you couldn't)
gardener, photographer, inventor.

My memory spools to your likeness as I knew it,
embraced by a Windsor chair
as the pall of Parkinson's rose to still
your legs
your hands
your lips
embalming your body but not your love of music.

So we played you songs,
your silence a backlit silhouette,
then kissed you goodbye,
the unrelenting stubble of your cheeks the dreaded prize.

Forty years hence
I snap a picture.
Cornstalks dwarf my son,
gardener, filmmaker, game designer.

And at day's end your voice
kisses me softly good night
(because it can)
incarnate through his hands
and the strings of your violin.

My Son Moves Out

I will never again
    wash farm-job socks
    dream to tunes plucked from mandolin
    find phone background changed overnight
    hear car coast into home's haven after night out
It's like coming to the end
of silk binding I've been fingering—
years of both wrinkles and tenderness
where loose threads now tassel
into something new

What Tendrils Hold

I want to ignore you, my pettiness, my timidity,
the agitation you cause, want to disappear

you—no hint of a backlit silhouette—
into some damask night. But you stare, plead

to your gods that I stay close, touch
even while I look away—like winter's sibling wolves

we tendril in our dissonance. Can my weeping
weaknesses glow in a beauty that comes

in curling close, filling cracks with fingered gold,
warming, despite snow's cold snarl?

Worries' Beads

If I could string my worries like beads
arrange the mismatched palette of forms
to a gratifying yet surprising pattern

I might choose to wear the bracelet
rub beads' pointed edges smooth
shine them with traces of day's rhymes
ice them when they fume and swell
threatening to bruise one another

I could leave them home one day
to tangle in a waiting box

or stand mid-bridge and break the string

Nana's Mirror

Looking into Nana's mirror—
silver hieroglyphed with years,
as I am now—I touch

the cracks, wounds etched
by neglect and its echoes.
My finger traces them, leaves

gold behind—filling,
mapping a yes to what
can yet be holy.

OVERNIGHT

Optical Possibilities

Are your eyes focused like mine
through lenses like butterflies'
wings? Either you spot sunrise
singing through stained glass or fail
to see past fractured, fragile
tissue paper, prone to burn,
dissolve under mere drizzle.

Cranes' View

Imagine the first
V of cranes
to ever split the sky
shrilling its *garooo*
headed across
bejeweled prairies
velveteen marshes
to winter wherever
warmth welcomed.

When the last
line of cranes
soars north
will its instinct
pinpoint the plot
allotted the species
as refuge?

hanging hopes from chandeliers IV

artwork by Bianca Artopé, 2016

I

How long could your family
with aunts
uncles
cousins
huddle in a room
with two neat beds
careful
not to tip
the lit candles
scratch the Scandinavian
furniture
smudge
the windows?
how long would you last
when the littlest ones require rocking
the elders fret
youngsters fuss
teenagers tire
the bathroom line winds
sighing through the night?

II

Dawn's colors crow
lovers grumble
sweat sours your breath
legs stretch
till feet annoy

III

And now your family
with aunts
uncles
cousins
needs to eat

A Kind of Nothing
Is Prominently There Instead

title from "Hay" by Maurice Manning

I hear a knot of jocularity
in morning birdsong
dream of sweet clover yet to bloom.
For you it's only worried birds
whose cares steep and stagnate
with yours as if in larvaed rain barrels.

I gasp at first spring blooms
kneel by Pheasant Eyes I planted
the day of Rhonda's surgery
reborn each spring as she was that May day.
For you the flower beds jeer with weeds
that paralyze your tidy mind.

I thrill at succulents swabbed soft with rain
that grow undaunted by stones
strewn on slope's canvas.
If only you could let them fill your day's page
instead of it being a kind of nothing
prominently there instead.

Languish, 2020

The wind brisk, we slipped
from the pre-covid shore
no sailor on board
our route unplotted

Now we languish, breezeless,
stare daily from steerage
into the same dank horizon
Questions huddle like clouds

Our hair hangs long   longer
and we've time enough
to braid it cable-strong
But why?

Today flower petals
wash in from somewhere
swirl then sink
their gift of perfume drowns

A dove sails past
salts our hopes for a harbor
where even stowaways
roam maskless,

vaccines spawn
no political fodder
and we can find our land legs
heady with the scent

of lilacs and lemons

In Gaza

one concert grand
and one music school

can't stitch the wounds
of thousands of greasy guns

of streets scalded by spite
families dismembered

of spring curfewed by fire
children's dreams gagged

But imagine Gaza
with just one gun

and thousands of pianos
playing as gently

as the first spring rain
filling a cup

that had forgotten
it could hold water

Overnight

the wind whipped so hard
that stars shivered   stones cowered

while silent breaths of will
just as inscrutable unfolded

the opaline petals
of my kitchen orchid

Managua por la mañana

Morning sounds in Managua
move my sleep towards light.
My dreams dawn to thoughts
as rooster's *kikirikí* inspires
tropical birds to trills as fanciful as their plumage.
Trucks labor uphill spewing
fumes and off-key fugues in their wake.
From behind the compound's scissor-wire-trimmed wall
our protector barks.
I should feel safe.
Against this backdrop enter voices
voices chanting slogans
voices marching in unison
under a choking cloud of smoking rubber.
My liminal senses perceive
reprise of revolution in Nicaragua
and fear sears my weary synapses.
Gathering courage I wake
and hear beyond the mirage
doves cooing in unison,
roosting above the embers
that warmed the poor of Managua
into tomorrow.
Mañana en Managua.

Weightless Wish

What I'd wish from Aladdin's
azure-brown lamp
is a cloud to wrap and lift me
for a swim in the sky
sleek with the mermaids
who sometimes skim
the sunset, heading east
even as rouge-tipped rays
singe their wayward tails.
I'd float with them
then turn
stroke
and turn again

fetters of the hopes
I'd had for myself
would unravel
weighing less
than breath

hanging hopes from chandeliers V

artwork by Bianca Artopé, 2016

Sun's rays target
us like lasers
Our bodies bond
wrapped to repel
sting
of sand and storm

Must our lives be stunted?
A smudged sum
of fear and greed?

Even as heat
wizens our sight
we plod toward
a place as sterile
as starkest winter

Let's imagine it dancing
awash in clever colors
welcoming
even our wounded warmth

Which Call, Which Kiss

Today I miss him
in the briskness
of rain's breeze
Home after long
day's drive
his voice over miles
would have warmed
against September
evening chill
as did comforts
whispered to a child
spending tears
for the cause of fairness
at her days' trailhead

We never know
which call, which kiss
will seal our story
like summer's lantana
weeping its last bloom
to the porch
uncelebrated

Ohio River Field Station

The hip boots are emptied of legs
and can do no more than stand
at ease, glazed with fishy smells
expectant of service in the war
to promote native fish
which host river mussel larvae
who become river-cleaning mussels
who stick out their fleshy
feet at hip boots who would
jump at the chance
to retire from service
and leave fish and mussels
to a victorious
symbiosis

Zoe's Example

When Zoe should fetch a
ball she brings back a branch
paws drip from her creek dip
quick illicit dip

When I strive for worthy words
others tumble to earth
weighted with broken bricks
acrid chipped bricks

Still others bubble acidic
corrode what tries to hold them
roil untamed in sinkholes
caustic stinking sinkholes

What would it take for Zoe
to leave her twig behind
for me to rainbow words through prisms
brilliant strings of prisms

All Brains and Thumbs

an arched branch fell
with the first winter storm,
now anchored by inch
after inch of snow—a cardinal's
perch where he awaits
a place at the feeder,
keeps clenched claws dry

if only I, with my brain-stuffed skull
and opposable thumbs could
grasp at chance as
firmly as he

EVERY DAY HAS
SOMETHING IN IT

Dear Joseph, December 16

Joseph Keeton Enzweiler, born December 18, 2020

Now that day's spring has unwound
in waiting, dear Joseph, rest
like red oak's marcescent leaves
still cradling December's snow
till time sighs and you, like them,
flutter astonished, awash
in breath of your lungs' making

The Sorcery of Sapphire Skies

found poem from Emily Dickinson's
"The skies cant keep their secret" (#213)

It is the sorcery
of sapphire skies
to overhear the secrets
of feckless hills
distill them to eyelet clouds
whisk them quickly
eastward then disperse
the whispers to fall
soft and seemingly
by chance

Redbuds, April 2020

Redbuds burst luminous
their profusion lights our journey
through drought-parched dreams.

Branches thatch a roof too low
for sadness to gather below.
Limbs linger just high enough
to lift eyes to

after we mourn each bud-gloved
twig the wind has whipped,
gloating, to the roadside.

Palimpsest

Ungainly starlings
gulp greedily at feeder
swarm in raucous flocks
sow sky-black panic
disrupt native
nuthatch   junco

But on year's
most dormant day
they bud thick like leaves
on bare branches
plumage sequined
as if by snowflakes
they seek to outfly

Suddenly wings rustle
like parchment
in thin wintry air

their grace a palimpsest
to preconception

Every Day Has Something in It

title from "Everything That Was
Broken" by Mary Oliver

not just the first glow of hope in the east
    golden sky becoming a canvas of stone-washed blue
not just birds who busy the sky
    mindful only of the task at hand

not just the sheep, the turtle, the tulip in azure sky
    sun pausing as noon's keystone
not just meadows garlanded with daisy and vetch
    fitted with thistle and cricket

not just the creek bank seeded with mink and crawdads
    and hill's dead ash tree the flicker covets
not just fresh-laid eggs that warm chilled hands
    the scent of sweet clover spilling into lungs

not just the sun descending through frescoed clouds
    toward dusk's invitation to lightning bugs
not just platoons of bats heralding night
    while Venus wakes under indigo sheets

Evening Mantra

Pour dusk's song like wax
from guttering candle
that leaves a hushed stripe

Listen to cat's drowsy breath
a stately Sarabande
accompanying flame's dance

Sense pendulum sway
in counterpoint
to cat's dreaming sleep

Knit and purl a wish to frame
and mount the moment
despite clock's mocking tick

Summer Tea

Trees gloved in green wave
like ladies from grand houses,
while others bow like farm hands

hungry for a sit-down snack.
They come with hats feathered
and chirping, twigs outstretched

like so many pinkies
or scarred with gnarls,
knotted by untold failures

and without much time
to dally over tea. Yet even
these last host in their boughs

a whistled tune or two,
promise a table weighted
with autumn's sweet abundance.

intrusion II

artwork by Bianca Artopé, 2017

sunset paints
her blue-gray voile
over high-rises
windows like rows

of robot eyes
reveal steel's zeal
for lifeless symmetry
of thought

but shards
of *ruach's* fire
light sandy causeways
where people flurry

barter words
comfort wounds
prospect for dreams
play at slumber

ignore the lock
of city lights

Providence

I

Spring will wake
escape from winter's cage

dimpled with birdsong
unbottling scent

of worm and bulb
through loam's lips

II

But this year
only yesterday

we hushed to hear the peepers
who should have lulled

February's twilight
and today April's phoebe

rasped her name
precocious by weeks

III

Spring will wake
reign above the fretting

over her capricious start
her court rising bedizened

from pristine pools
of providence

No Small Matter/*Keine Kleinigkeit*

found poem from Dorothea Haug's first letter
home after arriving in America in 1889

Cheerful morning boarding
No fear of storm   sandbank   thick fog
Evening comes
Then over and over tired night
Spent alone
Days turned upside down
Exhausted yearning
Till New York's unboarding
And one more night
Thank God
for cherry tree   chickens   next spring

Am Morgen heiter eingeschifft
Keine Angst vor Sturm   Sandbank   starkem Nebel
Der Abend kommt
Dann immer wieder müde Nacht
Allein zugebracht
Tage vollends umgeworfen
Erschöpfte Sehnsucht
Bis New Yorks Ausstieg
Und noch eine Nacht
Gott sei Dank
für Kirschbaum   Hühner   nächsten Frühling

Left Behind

I squat by the shelves
caught like a moth
in the dull-ocher book
Onkel Martin left behind.

I flutter past
gray-scale plates portraying
"The Door of Everlasting Life"
cast in Hildesheim, 1015

and alight on words,
letters my lips sound out:
Maria und das Kind.
My grandfather's vest

buttons smile, pulled
tight with pride
as I slit the chrysalis
of English

emerge yearning
for the language
his parents left behind.

Butterfly ballads

would tell of chrysalis
bondage, where darkness
blinds hides
the prize
of color sound flight
till the seam bursts
and crinkled, wet
carnelian wings
stretch and lean
into a song
in the key of dawn

Sometimes for a Moment

Sometimes for a moment
the air is as still as the sky is clear
But out of those unclocked seconds
the yellow-billed cuckoo calls
Pluck   pluck   pluck
as if elastic bands had bound
wind's breath

Then the firmament's
core uncurls
sap creeps up trunks
branches sway
cradle the still
unbrindled blue

About the Author

NANCY K. JENTSCH's chapbook *Authorized Visitors* (Cherry Grove Collections) and the collaborative chapbook *Frame and Mount the Sky* (Finishing Line Press), in which her poetry appears, were published in 2017. Since 2008, when she began writing, her work has appeared in both online and print journals such as *Amethyst Review, Eclectica, Panoply, Tiferet Journal,* and *Zingara Poetry Review,* and in numerous anthologies. In 2020 she received an Arts Enrichment Grant from the Kentucky Foundation for Women to work on this collection. She has retired after thirty-seven years of teaching at Northern Kentucky University and finds a bounty of inspiration for her writing in her family and their rural home.

SHANTI ARTS

NATURE • ART • SPIRIT

Please visit us online
to browse our entire book catalog,
including poetry collections and fiction,
books on travel, nature, healing, art,
photography, and more.

Also take a look at our highly regarded art
and literary journal, *Still Point Arts Quarterly*,
which may be downloaded for free.

www.shantiarts.com

CPSIA information can be obtained
at www.ICGtesting.com
Printed in the USA
BVHW042044081122
651445BV00009B/799

9 781956 056549